LA EXPERIENCIA DE UNA NINA

A TRAVÉS DE LA ADOPCIÓN

Michelle Lee Graham

La experiencia de una niña a través de la adopción

Editora: Alexa Tanen

Ilustradora: Yelyzaveta Serdyuk

Formato: Rocio Monroy

Fotógrafa: Stephanie Adkisson

Dedicado a mi primer nieto, Thomas Jeffrey.

Que siempre conozcas nuestra historia.

El reloj marcaba las 8:00 pm, era mi hora de dormir. Hora de comenzar la rutina nocturna de prepararme para ir a la cama, contar cuentos y decir las oraciones.

Me acurruqué en mis colchas
calientitas, los amorosos
ojos de mi mama viéndome,
—¿Me cuentas de nuevo sobre
cómo me amabas antes
de que me conocieras?

Me encantaba escuchar
sobre mi historia de adopción.

—Érase una vez, antes de que nacieras y mientras crecías en la pancita de otra mamá. Fuiste su primera bebé y eras muy especial para Michelle. Ella era todavía muy joven, pero ya te amaba con todo su ser.

—Tu papá y yo queríamos tener nuestro propio bebé. Entonces, oramos todos los días por un bebé a quien pudiéramos amar.

8

Al mismo tiempo, Michelle buscó por todas partes una mamá y un papá que pudieran darte todo lo que necesitabas. Este era su trabajo más importante como madre biológica y, con la ayuda de Dios, ¡nos convertimos en una familia!

Levanté las manos y sujeté su cuello con un gran y cálido abrazo, —¡Te amo, mami!

Más adelante, aprendí aún más acerca de la adopción cuando mi hermana, Lily, fue adoptada por nuestra familia. Me encantó convertirme en hermana mayor.

A medida que pasaban los años, a veces me preguntaba por mi madre biológica y mis otros hermanos y hermanas.
¿Cómo eran ellos?
Un día me encontré con una foto que nunca había visto antes.
Era de mi mamá biológica. Se parecía mucho a mí. Decidí buscarla.

El día que fui a visitarla me sentía muy emocionada.
Sabía que era familia y que me amaban.

Nuestra primera visita se prolongó hasta altas horas de la noche.
Yo no quería irme y Michelle tampoco quería que me fuera.
Nos abrazamos con fuerza. Cuando llegó el momento de
despedirnos, sabíamos que este era solo
el comienzo de nuestra vida juntas.

Con el paso de los años, siempre recuerdo lo mucho que fui amada desde el principio de mi vida.

15

El reloj marcaba las 8:00 pm, era hora de dormir para Tommy. Era hora de comenzar la rutina nocturna de prepararlo para ir a la cama, contar cuentos y decir nuestras oraciones.

Tommy se acurrucó en sus colchas calientitas,
sus brillantes ojos asomándose,
—Mami, ¿me cuentas un cuento antes de dormir?

Hice una pausa por un breve momento,
y con una pequeña sonrisa, comencé...
—Érase una vez, antes de que tú y yo naciéramos,
tu abuelito y abuelita habían estado orando por
tener un bebé propio...

Fin

ACERCA DE LA AUTORA

"Estoy orgullosa de ser una madre y compartir mi historia personal contigo"

Michelle Lee Graham

http://michelleleegraham.com/

OTROS LIBROS DE MICHELLE:

La experiencia de una madre biológica a través de la adopción. Experimenta el amor inquebrantable de una madre biológica por su hija. Conoce cómo navegó los años que siguieron al nacimiento de su hija y cómo compartió abiertamente su experiencia a través de la adopción con su familia. Finalmente, después de muchos años de esperanza y oración, se testigo de la historia de un reencuentro que hará que tu corazón se derrita. Un vínculo entre madre e hija que resistió la prueba del tiempo y que nunca se romperá.

OTROS LIBROS DE MICHELLE:

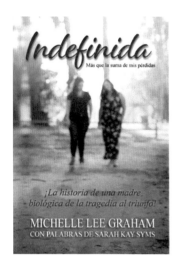

Todos los libros están disponibles en inglés

Disponibles en

Escanea el código para obtener tu propia copia

Lerner SPORTS

SPORTS

VIPs

MEET

PATRICK

MAHOMES

JOE LEVIT

Lerner Publications ◆ Minneapolis

SPORTS THRILLS MEET RESEARCH SKILLS

Lerner SPORTS

Free Database Trial: lernersports.com

Lerner Publications Company
An imprint of Lerner Publishing Group, Inc.
241 First Avenue North
Minneapolis, MN 55401 USA

For reading levels and more information, look up this title at www.lernerbooks.com.

Main body text set in Aptifer Slab Lt Pro. Typeface provided by Linotype AG.

Editor: Brianna Kaiser **Designer:** Kimberly Morales

Library of Congress Cataloging-in-Publication Data

Names: Levit, Joseph, author.
Title: Meet Patrick Mahomes / Joe Levit.
Description: Minneapolis : Lerner Publications, [2023] | Series: Sports VIPs (Lerner sports) | Includes bibliographical references and index. | Audience: Ages 7–11 | Audience: Grades 2–3 | Summary: "Quarterback Patrick Mahomes led the Kansas City Chiefs to Super Bowl victory in 2020. That year, he signed a record-breaking contract with the team. Learn about the superstar's life on and off the field"— Provided by publisher.
Identifiers: LCCN 2021042661 (print) | LCCN 2021042662 (ebook) | ISBN 9781728458144 (library binding) | ISBN 9781728463339 (paperback) | ISBN 9781728462318 (ebook)
Subjects: LCSH: Mahomes, Patrick, 1995– —Juvenile literature. | Football players—United States—Biography—Juvenile literature. | Quarterbacks (Football)—United States—Biography—Juvenile literature. | Kansas City Chiefs (Football team)—Juvenile literature.
Classification: LCC GV939.M284 L48 2023 (print) | LCC GV939.M284 (ebook) | DDC 796.332092 [B]—dc23

LC record available at https://lccn.loc.gov/2021042661
LC ebook record available at https://lccn.loc.gov/2021042662

Manufactured in the United States of America
3-1010378-50181-11/13/2023

TABLE OF CONTENTS

>>>>>>>>>>>>>>>>>>>>>

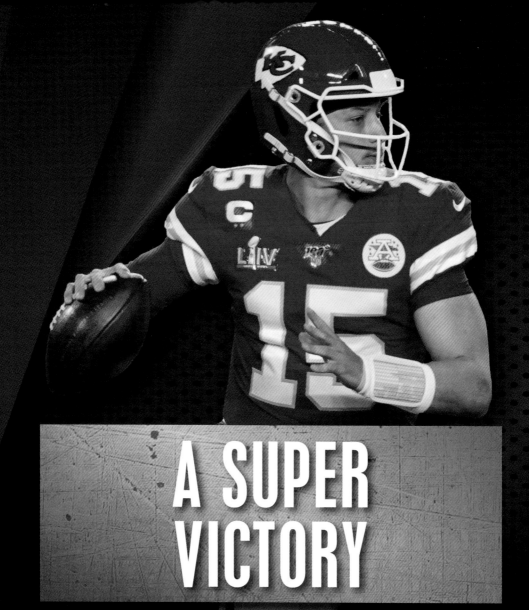

A SUPER VICTORY

On February 2, 2020, quarterback Patrick Mahomes and the Kansas City Chiefs faced the San Francisco 49ers in the Super Bowl. The score was tied 10–10 at halftime. In the third quarter, the 49ers scored 10 more points. The game was slipping away for the Chiefs.

In the fourth quarter, Mahomes knew it was now or never. With 7:13 left on the clock, he completed a 44-yard pass to wide receiver Tyreek Hill. The pass turned the Chiefs' luck around. "We never give up," Mahomes said. "The leaders that we have on this team, they have the mindset that we never give up and we're going to fight until the end." And they did.

FAST FACTS

DATE OF BIRTH: September 17, 1995
POSITION: quarterback
LEAGUE: National Football League (NFL)

PROFESSIONAL HIGHLIGHTS: helped the Kansas City Chiefs win the 2020 Super Bowl; named the 2020 Super Bowl Most Valuable Player (MVP); signed a 10-year contract with the Chiefs in 2020

PERSONAL HIGHLIGHTS: started a group called 15 and the Mahomies Foundation in 2019; became a part owner of the Kansas City Royals in 2020; became a father in 2021

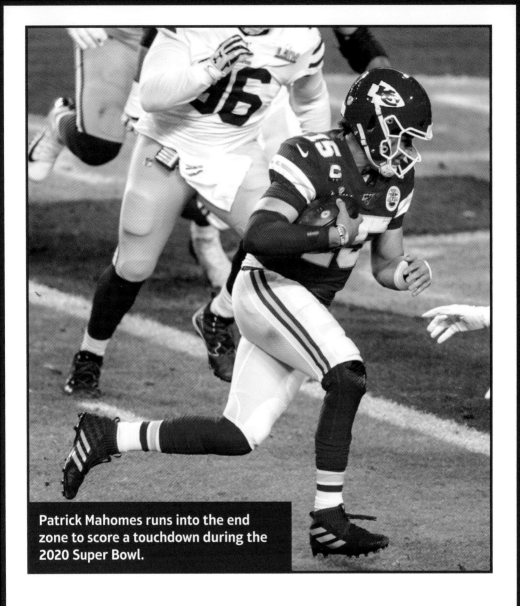

Patrick Mahomes runs into the end zone to score a touchdown during the 2020 Super Bowl.

In the last seven minutes of the game, Mahomes led the Chiefs to three touchdowns in a row. They took the lead and won the game 31–20. The Super Bowl was their first championship win in 50 years.

Mahomes won the Super Bowl MVP award. The 24-year-old was the youngest quarterback to win the award and the second youngest to win a Super Bowl.

Mahomes celebrates after helping the Chiefs win their second Super Bowl.

CHAPTER 1

AN AMAZING ATHLETE

Patrick Mahomes was born on September 17, 1995, in Tyler, Texas. His parents are Randi Mahomes and Patrick Mahomes Sr. He has three siblings: Jackson Mahomes, Zoe Mahomes, and Mia Randall.

Patrick's dad was a pitcher in Major League Baseball (MLB). Patrick grew up watching his dad and other pro baseball players practice. "I was in major-league clubhouses for pretty much my whole childhood," Patrick said. "You saw All-Stars working just as hard as guys who just got there." He learned that pro athletes must work really hard to be the best.

Pat Mahomes Sr. played 11 seasons in MLB.

Patrick participates in a practice with his father and the New York Mets in 2000.

Patrick was a baseball, basketball, and football star at Whitehouse High School in Texas. He later said that playing baseball and basketball helped him become a better football player.

As a senior, Patrick struck out 16 batters in a baseball game. But he really shined on the football field. He passed for 4,619 yards and 50 touchdowns. He also ran for 940 yards and 15 touchdowns.

Mahomes graduated from high school in 2014. MLB's Detroit Tigers picked him in the MLB Draft. But he wasn't ready to play pro sports. He went to college instead.

At Texas Tech, Mahomes played baseball and football for the Red Raiders. During his first football season, the Red Raiders had a 48–46 loss to Baylor. But Mahomes

Mahomes passes to Texas Tech receivers.

threw for a freshman-record 598 yards and six touchdowns in the game. Mahomes started in all 13 Texas Tech football games as a sophomore. He totaled 4,653 passing yards, 456 rushing yards, and 36 touchdowns that year.

As a junior, Mahomes turned his focus to football

Mahomes prepares to pass in a game against Texas Christian University.

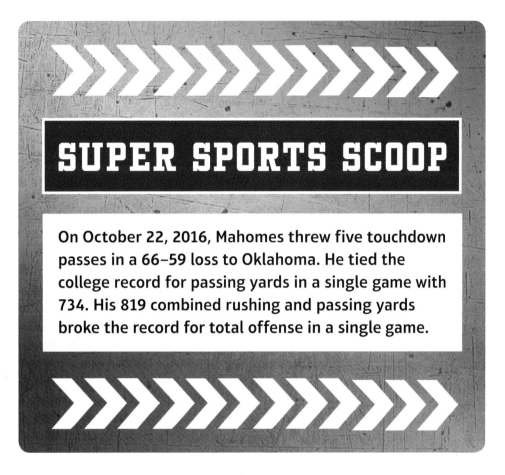

SUPER SPORTS SCOOP

On October 22, 2016, Mahomes threw five touchdown passes in a 66–59 loss to Oklahoma. He tied the college record for passing yards in a single game with 734. His 819 combined rushing and passing yards broke the record for total offense in a single game.

only. His college coach, Kliff Kingsbury, thought that was a good idea. "When he really focuses on football the majority of the time I think you're really going to see him take off in that position," Kingsbury said.

In 2016, Mahomes won the Sammy Baugh Trophy as the nation's top college passer. He led all college quarterbacks in yards per game (421), passing yards (5,052), and total touchdowns (53).

CHAPTER 2

ON THE BENCH

Mahomes was ready for the NFL after his junior year. At the 2017 NFL Scouting Combine, he tied the record for fastest pass ever recorded there. He zipped a throw at 60 miles (97 km) per hour!

The Chiefs badly wanted Mahomes. At the 2017 NFL Draft, they traded with the Buffalo Bills to receive the 10th overall pick. The Chiefs used it to select Mahomes.

First-round quarterbacks often play right away. But Kansas City head coach Andy Reid kept Alex Smith as the starter to give Mahomes time to gain experience. Sitting on the bench as a rookie made a difference for Mahomes.

Alex Smith (*left*) and Mahomes (*right*) stand on the sidelines during a game in 2017.

Mahomes runs with the ball during his career start in 2017.

SUPER SPORTS SCOOP

Mahomes had his first career start on December 31, 2017. He helped the Chiefs beat the Denver Broncos 27–24. He threw for 284 yards and completed 22 of 35 passes with one interception.

He watched the way Smith played and prepared for games. Smith helped him improve on his skills and prepare to be a strong starter.

CHAPTER 3

STAR QUARTERBACK

The Chiefs traded away Smith before the 2018 season.
The move made Mahomes Kansas City's leader on offense.
And he started out hot. He had 14 passing touchdowns
after four games.

At the end of the 2018 season, the Chiefs were 12–4. They were the top team in the American Football Conference (AFC). Mahomes became just the second quarterback after Dan Marino to pass for 5,000 yards and 50 touchdowns in a single season.

Mahomes looks to pass during a 2018 game against the Los Angeles Chargers.

The Chiefs faced the Indianapolis Colts in the first round of the playoffs. They crushed the Colts 31–13. In the AFC Championship, Mahomes passed for 295 yards and three touchdowns against the New England Patriots. But it wasn't enough. All-time great quarterback Tom Brady led the winning drive for the Patriots in overtime. Mahomes was disappointed, but he won the NFL MVP award for his great season.

Stretching before and after practices and games helps Mahomes keep his muscles healthy.

Mahomes (*left*) and Selena Gomez (*right*) join a celebrity softball game in 2019 to raise money for Children's Mercy Hospital.

Before the 2019 season, Mahomes worked hard to shake off the defeat. He trained in Texas at the Athlete Performance Enhancement Center. He stretched, lifted weights, and did other exercises to increase his strength and skills. He also started a group known as 15 and the Mahomies Foundation. It supports activities for kids such as sports and art.

Mahomes began the 2019 season with 10 touchdown passes and 1,510 passing yards in four games. But he injured his knee in week 7. He returned two weeks later and led the team to a second straight 12–4 regular-season record.

In the first round of the playoffs, the Chiefs were down 24–0 at the beginning of the second quarter

Mahomes looks to pass during a playoff game on January 12, 2020.

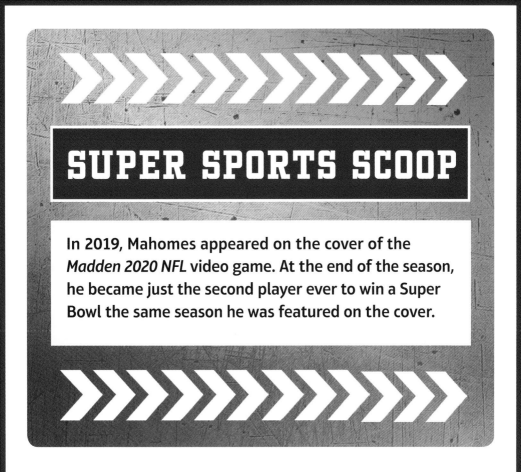

SUPER SPORTS SCOOP

In 2019, Mahomes appeared on the cover of the *Madden 2020 NFL* video game. At the end of the season, he became just the second player ever to win a Super Bowl the same season he was featured on the cover.

against the Houston Texans. Kansas City began to play better and scored 41 points to stomp the Texans 51–31. In the AFC Championship, the Chiefs fell behind again. Yet Mahomes led his team to a 35–24 victory over the Tennessee Titans.

The Chiefs came from behind once more in the Super Bowl. They scored 21 points in the fourth quarter to beat the 49ers. It was the team's second Super Bowl win.

CHAPTER 4

BACK TO THE SUPER BOWL

In the summer of 2020, Mahomes signed a 10-year contract with the Chiefs. The deal was worth up to $503 million. He was also busy in his personal life.

On September 1, 2020, Mahomes asked Brittany Matthews to marry him. Mahomes and Matthews had dated since high school. Matthews played pro soccer before becoming a personal trainer. The couple had their first child, Sterling Skye, in February 2021.

Matthews also helps Mahomes stay fit and eat healthful foods. Mahomes said, "I just try to eliminate some of the bad meals, the fast food, the foods that aren't great for your body." Eating healthful foods helps

Matthews and Mahomes watch a pro basketball game in 2019.

Mahomes build the extra muscle he needs to go up against NFL defenders.

Winning football games and breaking records has made Mahomes popular with companies. He endorses products like Oakley sunglasses and Adidas clothing. And in 2020, he became a part owner of the Kansas City Royals. That makes him a part of two pro teams in Kansas City.

Mahomes finished the 2020 regular season with 4,740 passing yards, 38 touchdowns, and only six interceptions. He suffered a head injury in the first round of the playoffs against the Cleveland Browns. But the Chiefs still won

Mahomes bats during a celebrity softball game in June 2019.

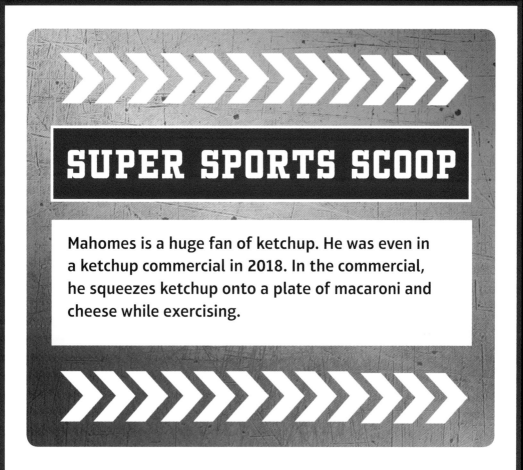

22–17. In the AFC Championship, he threw for 325 yards and three touchdowns to beat the Buffalo Bills 38–24.

In the Super Bowl, Tom Brady and the Tampa Bay Buccaneers beat the Chiefs 31–9. The Chiefs were missing several important players. And multiple Chiefs wide receivers dropped passes that could have been touchdowns. Still, Mahomes played well in a losing effort. Despite the setback, Mahomes has the will and the talent to become one of the NFL's greatest quarterbacks.

PATRICK MAHOMES CAREER STATS

GAMES STARTED:

57

PASSES ATTEMPTED:

2,136

PASSES COMPLETED:

1,408

PASSING TOUCHDOWNS:

139

PASSING YARDS:

17,352

INTERCEPTIONS:

35

GLOSSARY

draft: when teams take turns choosing new players

endorse: to recommend something, such as a product or service, usually in exchange for money

interception: a pass caught by the defending team that results in a change of possession

NFL Scouting Combine: a yearly event where football players display their skills for NFL teams

overtime: extra time added to a game when the score is tied at the end of the normal playing time

pro: short for professional, taking part in an activity to make money

regular season: when all the teams in a league play one another to determine playoff teams

rookie: a first-year player

starter: a player in the lineup at the beginning of a game

wide receiver: a football player whose main job is to catch passes

SOURCE NOTES

5 "Led by Patrick Mahomes, Chiefs Pull Off Epic Super Bowl Comeback," WRCB, February 3, 2020, https://www.wrcbtv.com /story/41643858/led-by-patrick-mahomes-chiefs-pull-off-epic -super-bowl-comeback.

9 Jenny Vrentas, "Patrick Mahomes Is Ready to Show Off His Fastball," *Sports Illustrated*, May 9, 2018, https://www.si.com /nfl/2018/05/09/patrick-mahomes-chiefs-andy-reid-alex-smith.

13 Betsy Blaney, "Texas Tech Gets Mahomes, Top In-State QB," Yahoo! News, February 5, 2014, https://www.yahoo.com/news /weather/texas-tech-gets-top-state-211544757--ncaaf.html.

25 Jacob Osborn, "Patrick Mahomes' Diet & Workout Plan," Man of Many, August 17, 2020, https://manofmany.com/lifestyle /fitness/patrick-mahomes-diet-workout-plan.

LEARN MORE

15 and the Mahomies Foundation
https://www.15andthemahomies.org

Kansas City Chiefs
https://www.chiefs.com

Levit, Joe. *Football's G.O.A.T.: Jim Brown, Tom Brady, and More.*
Minneapolis: Lerner Publications, 2020.

Scheff, Matt. *The Super Bowl: Football's Game of the Year.* Minneapolis:
Lerner Publications, 2021.

Sports Illustrated Kids—Football
https://www.sikids.com/football

Wetzel, Dan. *Patrick Mahomes.* New York: Henry Holt, 2020.

INDEX

PHOTO ACKNOWLEDGMENTS

Image credits: Robin Alam/Icon Sportswire/Getty Images, p. 4; Doug
Murray/Icon Sportswire/Getty Images, p. 6; AP Photo/Morry Gash, p. 7;
David Eulitt/Getty Images, p. 8; Jonathan Daniel/Allsport/Getty Images,
p. 9; AP Photo/Kathy Willens, p. 10; AP Photo/Icon Sportswire, p. 11; AP
Photo/Cal Sport Media, p. 12; AP Photo/Ed Zurga, p. 14; AP Photo/AJ Mast,
p. 15; AP Photo/Joe Mahoney, p. 16; Scott Winters/Icon Sportswire/Getty
Images, p. 18; AP Photo/Kevin Terrell, p. 19; Jamie Squire/Getty Images,
p. 20; Kyle Rivas/Getty Images, p. 21; Peter G. Aiken/Getty Images, p. 22;
Patrick Smith/Getty Images, p. 24; James Devaney/Getty Images, p. 25;
Ed Zurga/Getty Images, p. 26.

Cover image: AP Photo/Reed Hoffmann.